JIMMY BUFFETT
License to Chill

Project Managers: CAROL CUELLAR and AARON STANG
Transcribed by DANNY BEGELMAN
Music Editor: COLGAN BRYAN
Book Art Layout: LISA GREENE MANE
Album Artwork: © 2004 BMG Music

CONTENTS

Hey Good Lookin' 32
with CLINT BLACK, KENNY CHESNEY,
   ALAN JACKSON, TOBY KEITH and GEORGE STRAIT

Boats to Build. 24
with ALAN JACKSON

License to Chill 5
with KENNY CHESNEY

Coast of Carolina 16

Piece of Work 40
with TOBY KEITH

Anything Anytime Anywhere 10

Trip Around the Sun. 52
with MARTINA MCBRIDE

Simply Complicated 49

Coastal Confessions. 20

Sea of Heartbreak 60
with GEORGE STRAIT

Conky Tonkin' 27
with CLINT BLACK

Playin' the Loser Again 37
with BILL WITHERS

Window on the World 56

Someone I Used to Love. 64
with NANCI GRIFFITH

Scarlet Begonias. 44

Back to the Island 12

LICENSE TO CHILL

Slide Gtr. in Open G:
⑥ = D   ③ = G
⑤ = G   ② = B
④ = D   ① = D

Moderate shuffle ♩ = 128

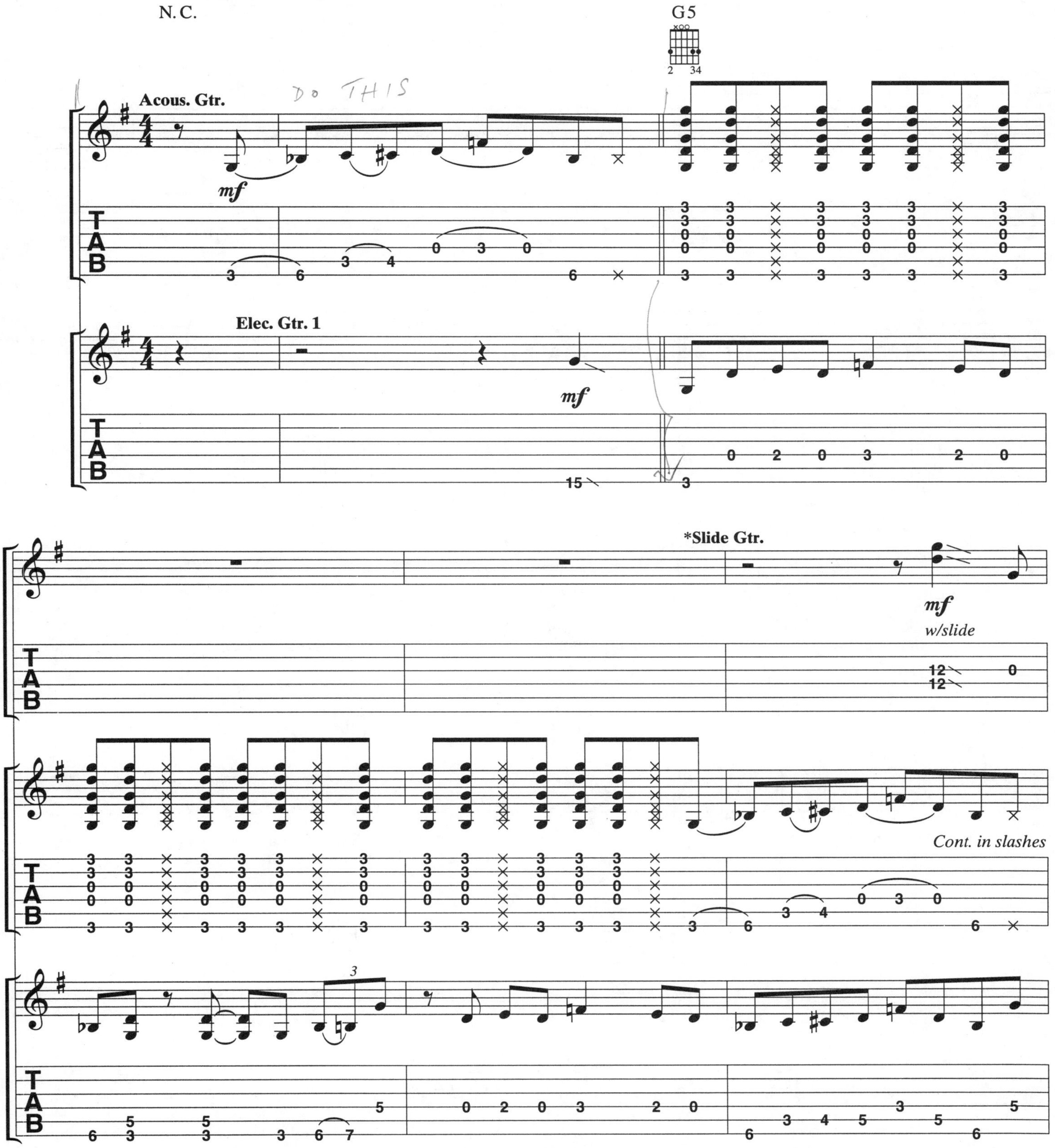

Words and Music by
JIMMY BUFFETT, MAC McANALLY
and AL ANDERSON

Verse:

1. Work, work, work, big pile__ of it and the boss is a jerk.__
2. Girls, girls, girls, ain't noth-in' like them in the whole wide_ world._ So

Just wan-na dis-ap-pear.__ And it's a-maz-ing what they pass off as a
damn smart and cute.__ Wish-in' I was some-where__

oth-er than__ here. Liv-in' for the week-end, jump right off the deep end with
bath-ing__ suit. Win-ners and__ los-ers, sail-ors and__ cruis-ers,__

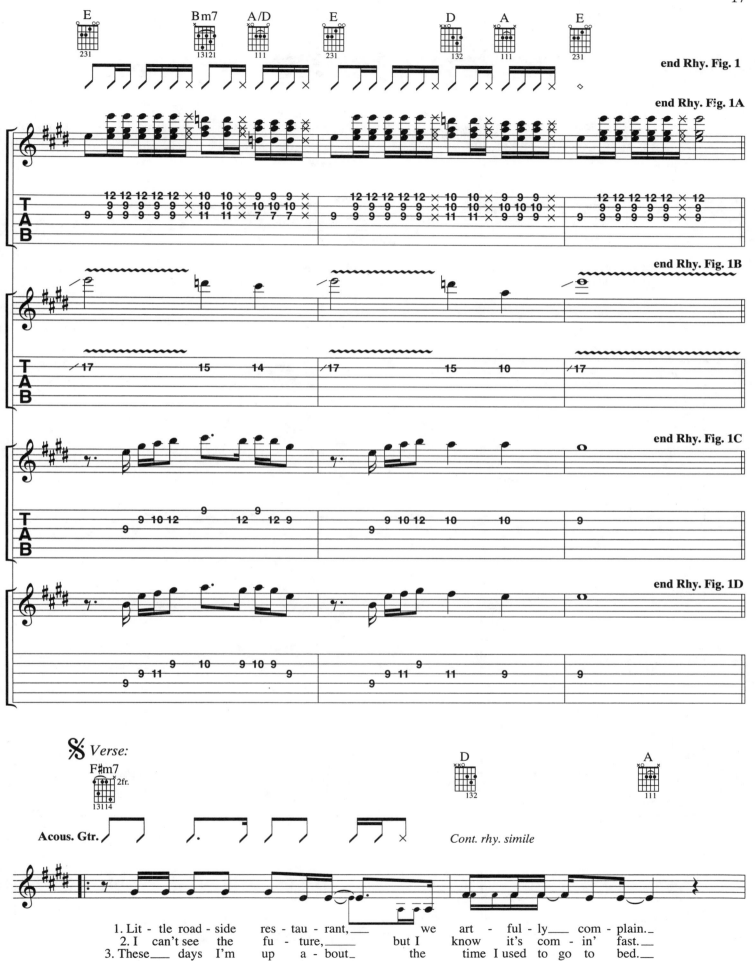

Coast of Carolina - 4 - 3
PGM0421

COASTAL CONFESSIONS

Slide Gtr. in Open E:
⑥ = E   ③ = G♯
⑤ = B   ② = B
④ = E   ① = E

Words and Music by
JIMMY BUFFETT

have me a boat__ drink or two.__ It's good for coast - al__ con - fes -

- sions, I hear.__ Tell the truth.__ Tell the truth.__ I've got some

coast - al__ con - fes - sions to make.__ How 'bout you?__ How__ 'bout

Outro: *Repeat and fade*
w/ad lib. vocal
w/ad lib. slide gtr. fills
(use gtr. solo as a
model for improv.)

you?   How 'bout you?   How__ 'bout you?

Verse 2:
Now, I'm a reader of the night sky, and a singer of inordinate tunes.
That's how I float across time, livin' way past my prime,
Like a long lost baby's balloon.
So, I hang on to the string, work that whole gravity thing.
But, when my spaceship goes pop, back to the earth I will drop,
Into the sea. or the limbs of a tree, or the wings of my love.
(To Chorus:)

Verse 3:
They say that time is like a river, and stories are the key to the past.
But, now I'm stuck in between, here at my typing machine,
Try'n' to come up with some words that will last.
It's so easy to see that we live history,
And if I just find the beat, I know I'll land on my feet.
I always do; hadn't got a clue.
Does it come from above?
(To Chorus:)

Verse 4:
So, let's talk about the future, or the consequences of my past.
I've got scars; I've got lines. I'm not hard to define;
Just an altar boy cov'rin' his ass.
I know I can't run and hide, but just hang on for the ride.
There will be laughter and tears as we progress through the years.
But, still, it's fun. Hey, I'm not done!
Gonna dance till I fall.
(To Coda / Chorus:)

BOATS TO BUILD

Words and Music by
GUY CLARK and
VERLON THOMPSON

Moderate calypso ♩ = 120
Intro:

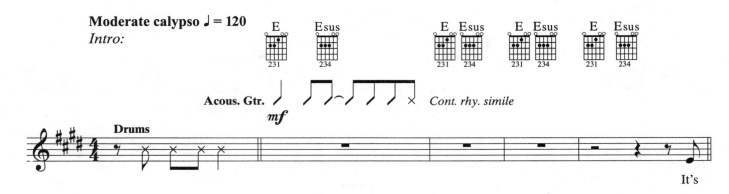

It's

Verse 1:

time for a change. I'm tired_____ of that same ol' same,_ the

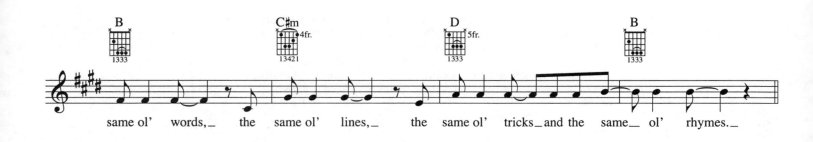

same ol' words,_ the same ol' lines,_ the same ol' tricks_and the same_ ol' rhymes._

Verses 2, 3, & 4:

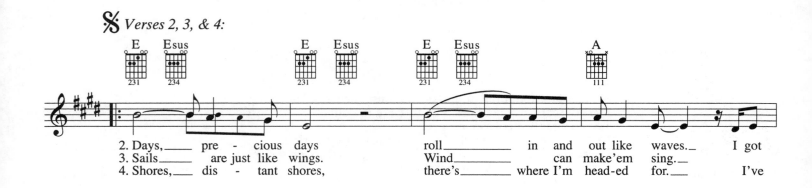

2. Days,_____ pre - cious days roll_____ in and out like waves._ I got
3. Sails_____ are just like wings. Wind_____ can make 'em sing._
4. Shores,_ dis - tant shores, there's_____ where I'm head-ed for._ I've

D.S. 𝄋 al Coda

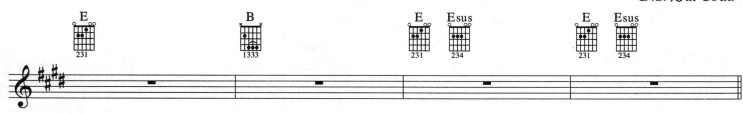

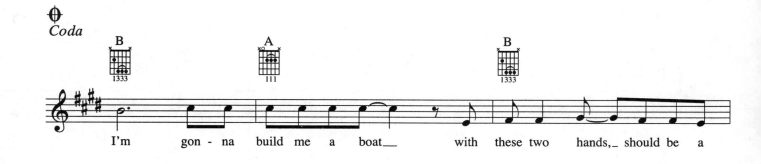

Coda

I'm gon - na build me a boat__ with these two hands,_ should be a

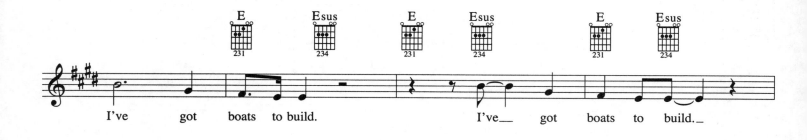

fair curve from a no - ble plan.__ Let the chips fall__ where they will__ 'cause

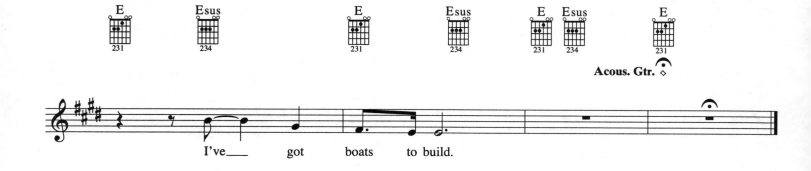

I've got boats to build. I've__ got boats to build.__

Acous. Gtr.

I've__ got boats to build.

CONKY TONKIN'

Words and Music by
JIMMY BUFFETT and
BINGO GUBELMAN

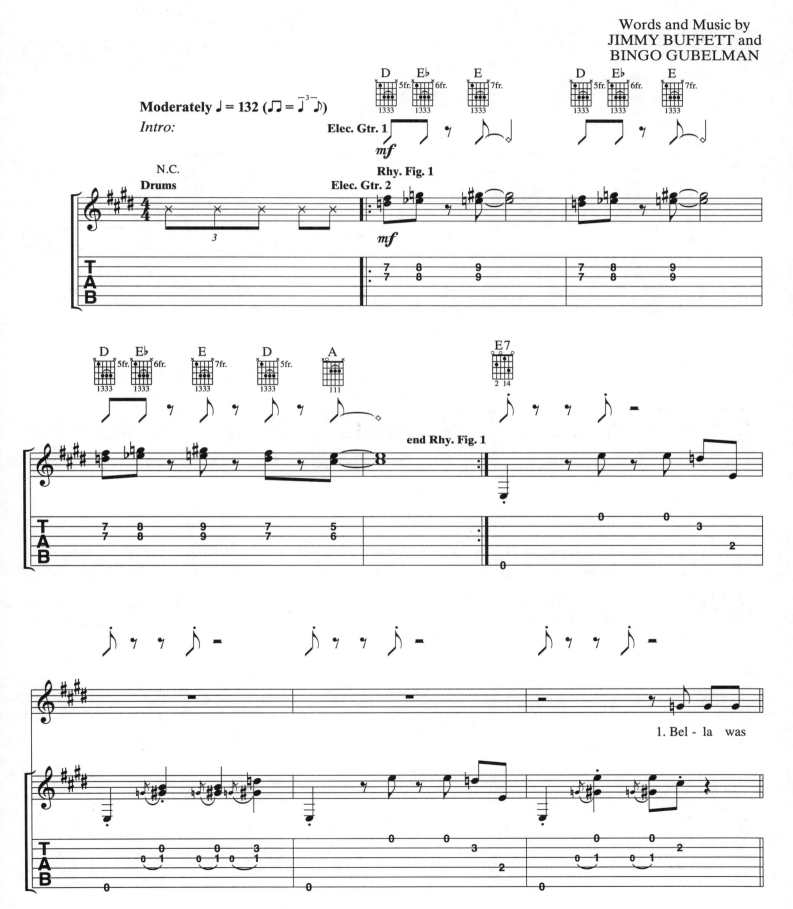

Verse:
Elec. Gtr. 2 w/ad lib. gtr. fills à la intro
E7
Cont. rhy. simile
bored to death with South Beach; not one ce - leb - ri - ty spot - ted in days.
2.3. See additional lyrics
She was tired of her mood, lunch - in' on ve - gan food. She was tired
of just soak - in' up rays.
A7
Then, she saw him pull up to the stop - light in an old rag - top that she could - n't name.
He said,
E7
To Coda
"Hop in - side. I'm head - in' south; take a ride. I'm just the next man that you're gon - na blame."
1.
B7
A7
U. S. One; head - in' down U. S.
E7
One.
2. Then he said,
2.
They're go - in'

30

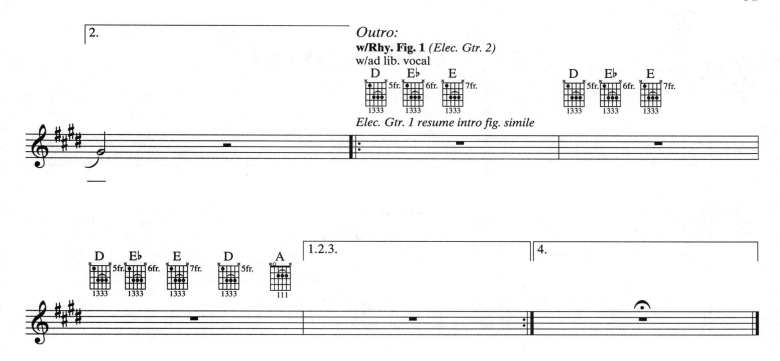

1.2.3.

4.

Verse 2:
Then he said, "How 'bout lunch in Key Largo?
There's a fish sandwich place down the road.
Kinda out in the sticks, but we can be back by six,
And never leave our area code."
Well, geography wasn't her strong point;
She'd never been past the Dadeland Mall.
So, they stopped on the way; Lenny was happy to pay
For her new thong and purple beach ball.
(To Chorus:)

Verse 3:
Somewhere in the middle of the Seven Mile Bridge,
He said, "Bella, do you wanna see the rest?"
She said, "I haven't a care, Lenny; just take me there."
And they drove all the way to Key West.
Well, she'd never seen anything like it
In all of her twenty-six years.
Bella was feelin' the groove; Lenny was makin' his move.
They were quite a pair of pioneers.
(To Chorus:)

HEY GOOD LOOKIN'

Words and Music by
HANK WILLIAMS

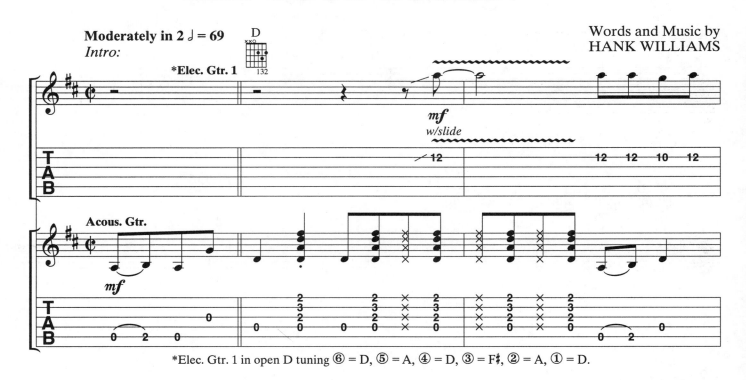

*Elec. Gtr. 1 in open D tuning ⑥ = D, ⑤ = A, ④ = D, ③ = F♯, ② = A, ① = D.

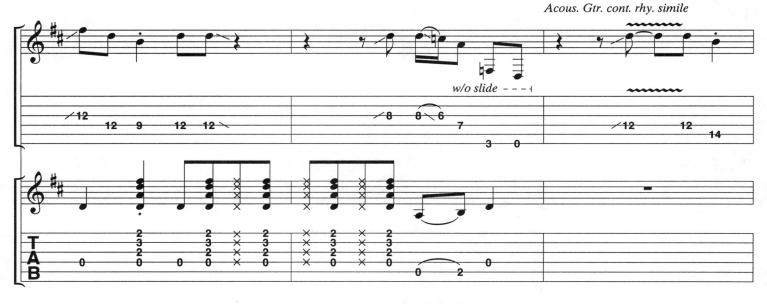

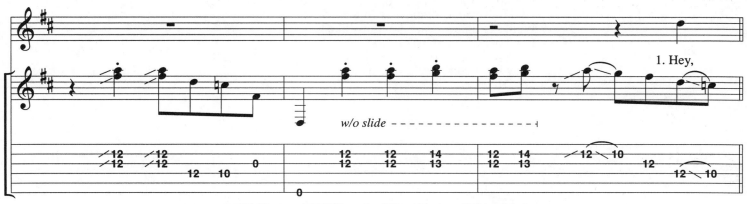

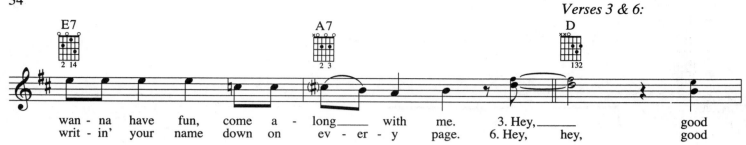

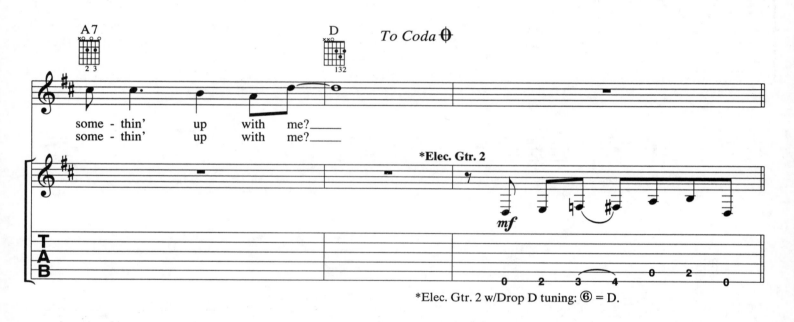

*Elec. Gtr. 2 w/Drop D tuning: ⑥ = D.

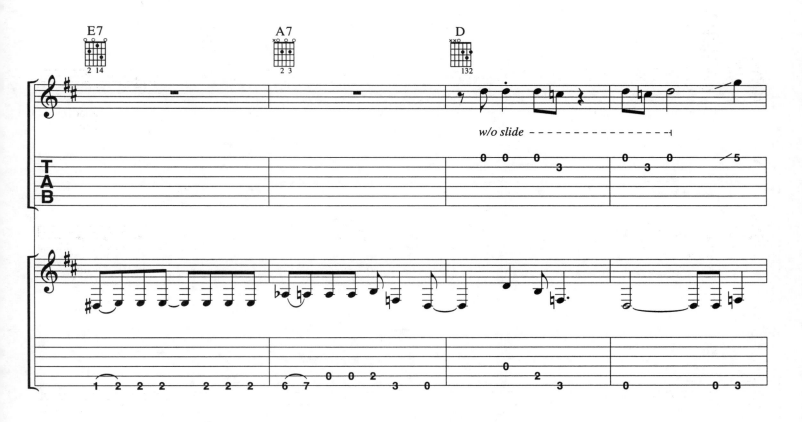

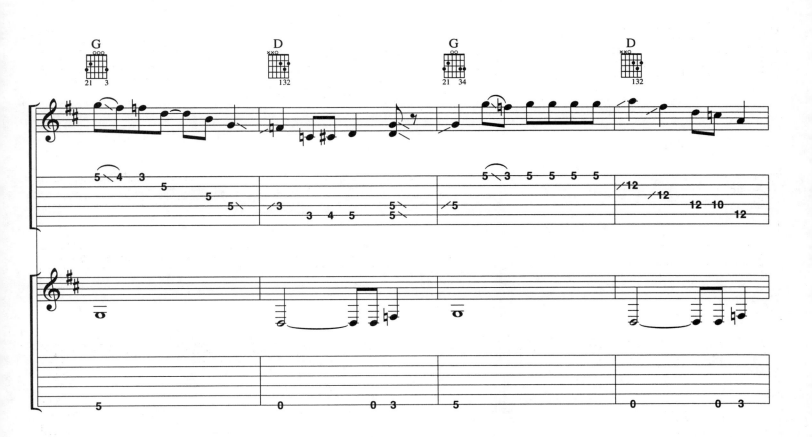

PLAYIN' THE LOSER AGAIN

Words and Music by
BILL WITHERS

PIECE OF WORK

Words and Music by
WILLIAM A. KIMBROUGH

piece of work,— I'm i-ron and lace, I'm shy right up there in your face. I'm

all dumb-found-ed, stub-born as an ass, sharp as an ar-row in a pile of glass. I'm a

Coda

I'm a piece of work,___ I'm a piece of work,___ I'm a piece of work.___

Outro:
w/ad lib. Slide Gtr. fills (use Interlude as a model for improv.)

E5

Repeat and fade

Verse 3:
I'm a piece of work, I'm an angel's fiend,
Bathed in lavender and gasoline.
Scared brave, shallow in an ink-black well,
Lightly browned in the fires of hell.
Wicked, holy, full-on fake,
Best known for my big mistake.
I'm a zen-wise peaceful gone berserk,
Good God Almighty, I'm a piece of work.

Verse 4:
I'm a dreadful sight and I just don't care,
Spent all morning pulling out my hair.
I woke at dawn with a crazy spin,
Half the day trying to glue back in.
Mother, Bloody Mary, please,
Wipe that smile right off your knees.
I'm the CEO of the mailroom clerks,
Lord, have mercy, what a piece of work.
(To Interlude:)

Verse 5:
I'm a piece of work, I'm a lovesick boy,
Cloth cap, caviar and corduroy.
All over the map, just lost in space,
With a filthy mind and a choirboy's face.
Heels up, head down, straight on through,
Watch out, woman, I'm-a get to you.
I'm a gladiator with a mind to irk,
Good God Almighty, I'm a piece of work.
(To Coda)

SCARLET BEGONIAS

Words and Music by
JEROME GARCIA
and ROBERT HUNTER

*Chords are suggested.

Scarlet Begonias - 5 - 2
PGM0421

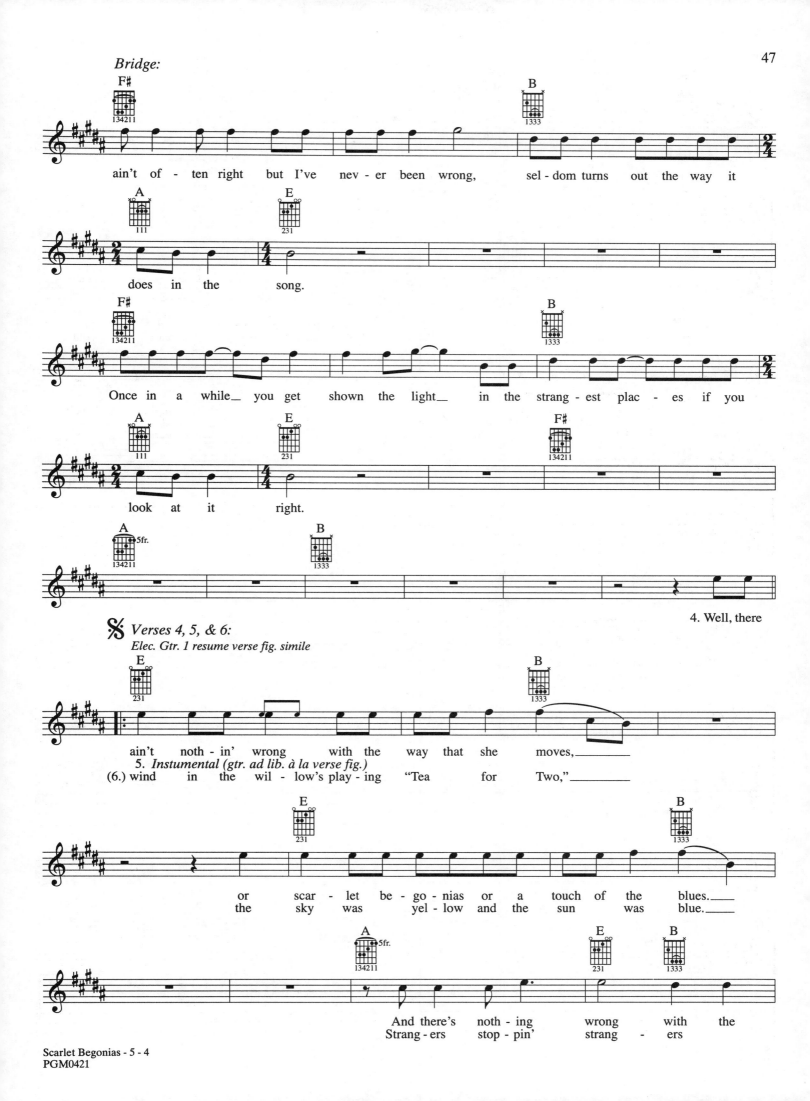

Bridge:

ain't of - ten right but I've nev - er been wrong, sel - dom turns out the way it

does in the song.

Once in a while__ you get shown the light__ in the strang - est plac - es if you

look at it right.

4. Well, there

Verses 4, 5, & 6:
Elec. Gtr. 1 resume verse fig. simile

ain't noth - in' wrong with the way that she moves,_____
5. *Instumental (gtr. ad lib. à la verse fig.)*
(6.) wind in the wil - low's play - ing "Tea for Two,"_____

or scar - let be - go - nias or a touch of the blues.____
the sky was yel - low and the sun was blue.____

And there's noth - ing wrong with the
Strang - ers stop - pin' strang - ers

SIMPLY COMPLICATED

Words and Music by
JIMMY BUFFETT
and BILL WITHERS

Verses 2 & 4:

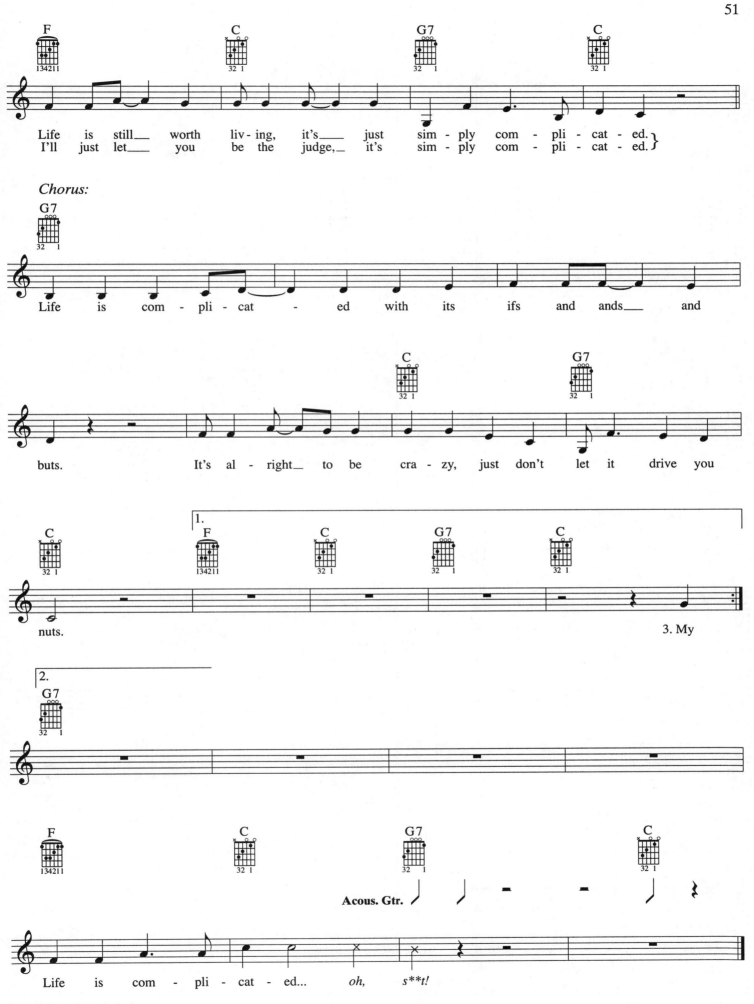

Life is still__ worth liv - ing, it's__ just sim - ply com - pli - cat - ed.
I'll just let__ you be the judge, it's sim - ply com - pli - cat - ed.

Chorus:

Life is com - pli - cat - ed with its ifs and ands__ and

buts. It's al - right__ to be cra - zy, just don't let it drive you

1.
nuts. 3. My

2.

Life is com - pli - cat - ed... *oh, s**t!*

Acous. Gtr.

TRIP AROUND THE SUN

Words and Music by
AL ANDERSON, STEVE BRUTON
and SHARON VAUGHN

WINDOW ON THE WORLD

Words and Music by
JOHN HIATT

Elec. Gtr. in Open D w/capo II:
⑥ = D ③ = F♯
⑤ = A ② = A
④ = D ① = D

Moderately ♩ = 120
Intro:

Acous. Gtr. w/capo II

Cont. rhy. simile

*TAB numbers relative to capo.

Verses 1 & 3:

1. A bro-ken prom-ise I kept too long,— a greas-y shade and a
3. In broad day-light that cir-cus tent,— pulled up stakes, I don't know

cur-tain drawn,— a bro-ken glass and a heart gone wrong:
where it went.— A closed dark room with a bust-ed vent,—

𝄋 *Verses 2, 4, & 5:*

that's my win-dow on the world.
that's my win-dow on the world.

2. A cup of cof-fee in a
4. I think a-bout you when I'm
5. Down on In-di-an-a

Window on the World - 4 - 1
PGM0421

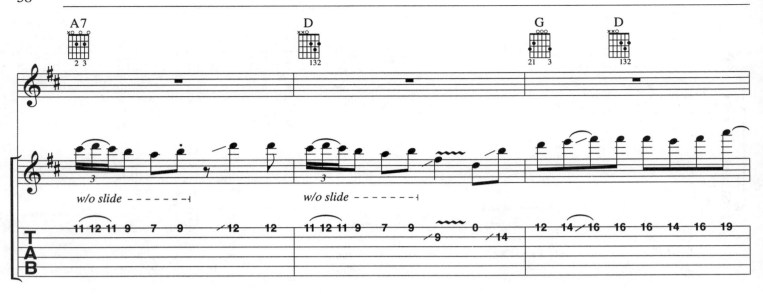

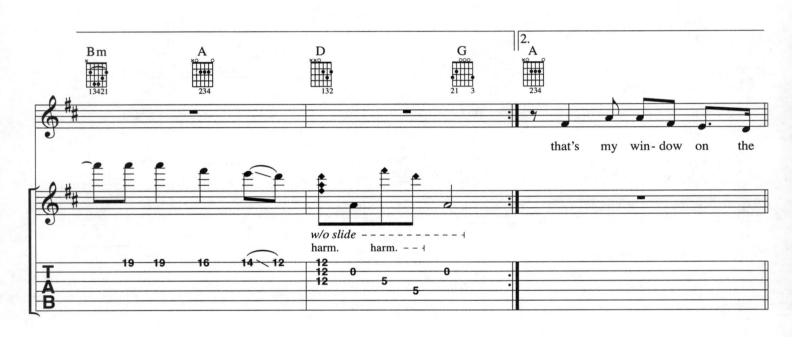

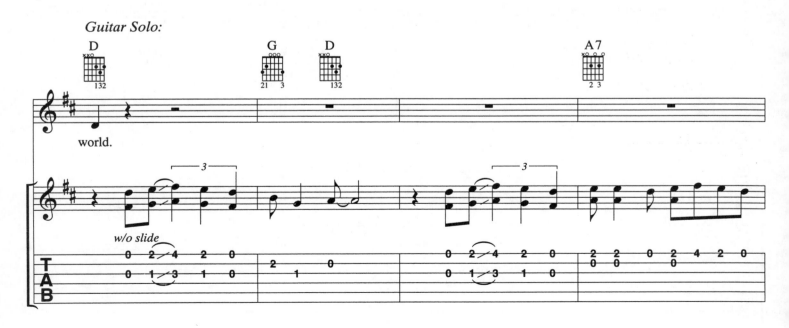

SEA OF HEARTBREAK

Words and Music by
HAL DAVID and PAUL HAMPTON

62

SOMEONE I USED TO LOVE

Acous. Gtr. Capo II

Moderately ♩ = 84

Words and Music by
BRUCE COCKBURN

*To match record key capo at second fret.

Someone I Used to Love - 3 - 1
PGM0421

Interlude:
Violin Solo:

Pedal Steel Gtr. Solo:

D.S. 𝄋 *al Coda*

3. This

⊕
Coda

rit.

GUITAR TAB GLOSSARY **

TABLATURE EXPLANATION

READING TABLATURE: Tablature illustrates the six strings of the guitar. Notes and chords are indicated by the placement of fret numbers on a given string(s).

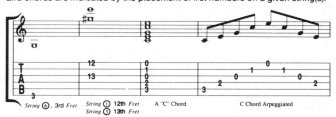

String ⑥ , 3rd Fret   *String* ① 12th Fret   A "C" Chord   C Chord Arpeggiated
String ③ 13th Fret

BENDING NOTES

 HALF STEP: Play the note and bend string one half step.*

 **WHOLE STEP:** Play the note and bend string one whole step.

 **WHOLE STEP AND A HALF:** Play the note and bend string a whole step and a half.

SLIGHT BEND (Microtone): Play the note and bend string slightly to the equivalent of half a fret.

 **PREBEND (Ghost Bend):** Bend to the specified note, before the string is picked.

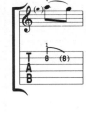 **PREBEND AND RELEASE:** Bend the string, play it, then release to the original note.

 **REVERSE BEND:** Play the already-bent string, then immediately drop it down to the fretted note.

BEND AND RELEASE: Play the note and gradually bend to the next pitch, then release to the original note. Only the first note is attacked.

*A half step is the smallest interval in Western music; it is equal to one fret. A whole step equals two frets.

UNISON BEND: Play both notes and immediately bend the lower note to the same pitch as the higher note.

 **DOUBLE NOTE BEND:** Play both notes and immediately bend both strings simultaneously.

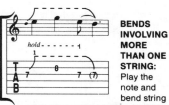 **BENDS INVOLVING MORE THAN ONE STRING:** Play the note and bend string while playing an additional note (or notes) on another string(s). Upon release, relieve pressure from additional note(s), causing original note to sound alone.

 **BENDS INVOLVING STATIONARY NOTES:** Play notes and bend lower pitch, then hold until release begins (indicated at the point where line becomes solid).

TREMOLO BAR

 **SPECIFIED INTERVAL:** The pitch of a note or chord is lowered to a specified interval and then may or may not return to the original pitch. The activity of the tremolo bar is graphically represented by peaks and valleys.

 **UN-SPECIFIED INTERVAL:** The pitch of a note or a chord is lowered to an unspecified interval.

HARMONICS

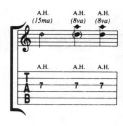 **NATURAL HARMONIC:** A finger of the fret hand lightly touches the note or notes indicated in the tab and is played by the pick hand.

ARTIFICIAL HARMONIC: The first tab number is fretted, then the pick hand produces the harmonic by using a finger to lightly touch the same string at the second tab number (in parenthesis) and is then picked by another finger.

 **ARTIFICIAL "PINCH" HARMONIC:** A note is fretted as indicated by the tab, then the pick hand produces the harmonic by squeezing the pick firmly while using the tip of the index finger in the pick attack. If parenthesis are found around the fretted note, it does not sound. No parenthesis means both the fretted note and A.H. are heard simultaneously.

**By Kenn Chipkin and Aaron Stang

RHYTHM SLASHES

STRUM INDICATIONS: Strum with indicated rhythm.

The chord voicings are found on the first page of the transcription underneath the song title.

INDICATING SINGLE NOTES USING RHYTHM SLASHES: Very often single notes are incorporated into a rhythm part. The note name is indicated above the rhythm slash with a fret number and a string indication.

ARTICULATIONS

HAMMER ON: Play lower note, then "hammer on" to higher note with another finger. Only the first note is attacked.

LEFT HAND HAMMER: Hammer on the first note played on each string with the left hand.

PULL OFF: Play higher note, then "pull off" to lower note with another finger. Only the first note is attacked.

FRETBOARD TAPPING: "Tap" onto the note indicated by + with a finger of the pick hand, then pull off to the following note held by the fret hand.

TAP SLIDE: Same as fretboard tapping, but the tapped note is slid randomly up the fretboard, then pulled off to the following note.

BEND AND TAP TECHNIQUE: Play note and bend to specified interval. While holding bend, tap onto note indicated.

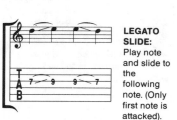

LEGATO SLIDE: Play note and slide to the following note. (Only first note is attacked).

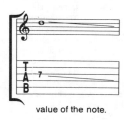

LONG GLISSANDO: Play note and slide in specified direction for the full value of the note.

SHORT GLISSANDO: Play note for its full value and slide in specified direction at the last possible moment.

PICK SLIDE: Slide the edge of the pick in specified direction across the length of the string(s).

MUTED STRINGS: A percussive sound is made by laying the fret hand across all six strings while pick hand strikes specified area (low, mid, high strings).

PALM MUTE: The note or notes are muted by the palm of the pick hand by lightly touching the string(s) near the bridge.

TREMOLO PICKING: The note or notes are picked as fast as possible.

TRILL: Hammer on and pull off consecutively and as fast as possible between the original note and the grace note.

ACCENT: Notes or chords are to be played with added emphasis.

STACCATO (Detached Notes): Notes or chords are to be played roughly half their actual value and with separation.

DOWN STROKES AND UPSTROKES: Notes or chords are to be played with either a downstroke (⊓) or upstroke (∨) of the pick.

VIBRATO: The pitch of a note is varied by a rapid shaking of the fret hand finger, wrist, and forearm.